Favor Now!

How to Live in the Favor of God

Bruce Lindley

Foreword by Pamela A. Segneri

"Favor Now - How to Live in the Favor of God" by Bruce Lindley

Copyright © 2025 Bruce Lindley

Published by ARC Global PO Box 3398, Helensvale B.C. QLD 4212, Australia

This book or parts thereof may not be reproduced in any form, stored in a retrieval system, or transmitted in any form by any means – electronic, mechanical, photocopy, recording or otherwise – without prior written permission of the publisher, except as provided by Australian copyright law.

Unless otherwise noted, scripture quotations are taken from The Holy Bible, New International Version®, NIV®. Copyright © 1973, 1978, 1984, 2011 by Biblica, Inc. Used with permission of Zondervan. All rights reserved worldwide. www.zondervan.com

All rights reserved worldwide. The "NIV" and "New International Version" are trademarks registered in the United States Patent and Trademark Office by Biblica, Inc.™

Scripture quotations marked (Amplified) are taken from the Amplified® Bible (AMP), Copyright © 1954, 1958, 1962, 1964, 1965, 1987 by The Lockman Foundation. Used by permission

Scripture quotations marked (TPT) are from The Passion Translation®.

Copyright © 2017, 2018, 2020 by Passion & Fire Ministries, Inc. Used by permission. All rights reserved. ThePassionTranslation.com

Scripture quotations marked (NLT) taken from Holy Bible. New Living Translation Copyright© 1996, 2004, 2007, 2013 by Tyndale House Foundation. Used by permission of Tyndale House Publishers Inc., Carol Stream, Illinois 60188. All rights reserved.

Scripture quotations marked (NKJV) taken from the New King James Version®. Copyright © 1982 by Thomas Nelson. Used by permission. All rights reserved.

Cover Design by Rachel LeRoux.

Editing and Layout by Mountain Train Media

Printed in Australia   ISBN: 978-0-6450498-2-4

2 Corinthians 6:2

*For he says, "In the time of my favor I heard you,
and in the day of salvation, I helped you."
I tell you, now is the time of God's favor,
now is the day of salvation*

Dedication

Favor Now - How to Live in the Favor of God is dedicated to our Lord Jesus Christ who radically changed my life 50 years ago! I have never been same. I am eternally grateful for your grace, salvation and favor in my life. Your favor and blessing each day still surprises and astounds me.

This is also dedicated to my amazing wife Cheryl and our wonderful family. You are the greatest demonstration of the favor of God in my life. What joy it is to live for Jesus together!

And I dedicate this book to the remarkable apostles and prophets in our apostolic community ARC Global. God's favor has brought us into relationship and to build the Kingdom of God together. What a joy to have you in our lives.

All of you are a demonstration of the Favor of God in my life – Now!

Acknowledgements

This book wouldn't have been possible without the support and help of my amazing wife Cheryl Lindley. You are an ongoing inspiration and blessing to me.

Thank you to the remarkable Paul Segneri who continues to bless us and our ministry. You are a gift to us and the kingdom of God.

A special thank you to Pamela A. Segneri for the honor it is to have her writing the Foreword of this book. You are such a blessing to us. We are so grateful to God for you and Paul and for your ongoing friendship and love.

Contents

Foreword – Pamela A. Segneri	p11
Introduction	p15
Chapter 1 - Why is Favor so Important?	p21
Chapter 2 - What does God's Favor Look Like?	p29
Chapter 3 - Living in the Favor of God TODAY	p43
Chapter 4 - Next Level Favor Operating System	p55
Chapter 5 - Blessed and Highly Favored	p73
Chapter 6 - Blessing and Favor in the Spacious Place	p87
Chapter 7 - The Time is Now	p101
Chapter 8 - Expecting the Favor of God Every Day	p113
Conclusion - My Final Favor Words for You	p121
Appendices	
Appendix 1 - Favor Scriptures in the Bible	p125
Appendix 2 - Favor Decrees	p135
Appendix 3 - Your Salvation Prayer Today	p137
Endnotes	p141
Contact and Resource Details	p147
Connect with ARC Global	p151

FOREWORD

Wow, Favor Now!

The favor of God is exciting and we should all want it. I would like to stress this is not the latest fad whereby if you get this all will be well with everything in your life. No, this is not a fad! The divine <u>favor</u> of God was in Genesis and is still available today. The point of difference is that Bruce Lindley skilfully weaves favor with faith, obedience, revelation of the Word and prayer. None of these blessings that salvation in Christ gives us access to stand alone, they all play an important and necessary part of a fulfilled life as a believer in Jesus Christ. He gave us a complete package, a complete blessing.

In this book Bruce steps us through every facet of the Favor of God but doesn't leave us there, he provides us with the road map to live in it. The encouragement to search the scriptures and meditate on them allowing the Word to become flesh in us and endure through our lives is priceless. So many times good ideas have left us wondering how do I get from here to there - this anointed work steps us carefully into the fulness of God's promise.

This book is fresh and very timely. The testimonies of Bruce and Cheryl's lives are real, however, not unique to them - follow the road map and you will have your own testimony of the favour of God in your life. As people's conversations seem to be around the increasing cost of living, house prices and pretty much anything that costs money - it's refreshing to be reminded that we are highly favored of God. We are His kids and He will always have us front and centre of His thoughts and decision making. As we cultivate our intimate relationship with our Father God His favor flows.

Please remember this is not about work, it's all about intimate relationship with our heavenly Father who loves us. It is one thing to intellectually know that and quite another to live in it. It's the living, it's the abiding in that Word which keeps us in what I like to call our 'God Bubble'.

I love that Bruce has included Favor Decrees Job 22:28 "You will also decree a thing and it will be established for you. And light will shine on your ways". Your decrees can keep your faith focussed, they are a powerful reminder to ourselves. As we speak them out, see them going out into the spirit realm bringing things which have been out of line back under the Lordship of Christ Jesus. As His favour flows in our lives we are no longer 'under the circumstances'. We are the circumstance!

This book is a keeper! I know you will reread it over and over as you get this truth into your spirit. Be challenged, be inspired and be in the flow of God's Favor.

I am not sure if I am the friend Bruce was referring to when

INTRODUCTION

he said he had a friend who always said they were God's favorite (cos I have been saying that for years) - however, you can be God's Favorite too!

I am delighted to write this foreword as an endorsement and also a recommendation of Favor Now! I would also commend to you our brother Bruce Lindley. My husband Paul and I have walked through many things with Bruce and Cheryl and I am delighted to report we travelled through them, we did not camp as we are on our way to our destiny. Bruce is truly an Apostolic Father, his heart is for the body of Christ to live in everything God has provided. God is audacious and I believe He wants our faith to receive His Favor to be audacious!

Pamela A. Segneri

Co-Founder Integrity Restoration Ministries

Co-Founder and Presenter firestartersTV

Author

H.I.M. & A.R.C. Apostle

Introduction

Does God really want to give you 'FAVOR'? Yes!

Favor is much more than the blessing of God. It is part of His free gift of grace to you.

Through Christ, FAVOR is available to you NOW!

2 Corinthians 6:2 says

> *For he says, "In the time of my favor I heard you, and in the day of salvation, I helped you." **I tell you, now is the time of God's favor...***

Welcome to a journey of discovering and living in a greater level of God's favor TODAY – NOW!

Favor is found repeatedly in the Bible – from Genesis right through the Old and New Testaments. God is an amazing Father! When you know the love of the Father, it is Father's Day every day. Why is this important? Because when you truly know the Father, you will experience the blessing of His favor.

We have five children. They are ALL my favorites – not just one of them.

Why? Every good father wants to bless all His children. This includes showing them favor!

When two of our daughters were first married they were both saving to buy their first home. We knew that it was going to take at least 10 years for them to save a deposit to do that themselves. It seemed to be more difficult for them as the house prices kept increasing. So, my wife and I borrowed more from our house loan to give our daughter's the head start they needed. It cost us to bless our children with their house deposit. We sacrificed so they could have an opportunity to establish their own lives. As a result, they were both able to buy their first home.

Why did we do that? We showed favor to our children. God will show favor to you too!

In Matthew 7:10-11 Jesus said

> *Which of you, if your son asks for bread, will give him a stone? Or if he asks for a fish, will give him a snake? If you, then, though you are evil, know how to give good gifts to your children, how much more will your Father in heaven give good gifts to those who ask him!*

Fathers and mothers desire to bless their children with 'good

INTRODUCTION

gifts' even if it costs them greatly.

Growing up, I was the oldest of three boys. As teenagers we were always hungry. So much so that our parents became the local butcher's best customer. I know that because when my dad was transferred to another city the local butcher cried when he heard the news. Our evening meal was always the largest. Even though my mother was a good cook and cooked large amounts of food so our plates were full, she could never seem to fill us up.

Over and over again I remember, after we'd eaten our first serving, we'd asked was there any more food, she would say 'Here have mine, I am not hungry' and quietly offer her dinner for us to eat.

Years later after I became a father, I was feeding my children, and it dawned on me that my mother was hungry and that she quietly sacrificed her own need for food to fill her growing sons. When I asked her about it, she smiled and said, 'Yes I was hungry, but that's what parents do!'

Fathers and mothers sacrifice for their sons and daughters.

God the Father also does that for us!

Why? Because we are His favorite!

Scripture says that we indeed are 'the apple of His eye'. [1]

I have a friend that would always say that she was God's favorite. It used to bug me, so I went looking in the Bible. Guess what – She was right!

She is God's favorite! But so are you!
In fact, we are ALL are His favorites.

The good news is that the 'favor of God' has many layers to it. So much so you will be blessed as you grow in your understanding and step into the fullness of the 'Favor of God'.

The favor of God is not just meant for us to enjoy!
It has a divine purpose that will unlock your God destiny and place you in the presence of others to transform their lives.

We have been traveling to Kenya for many years to equip pastors and leaders. On one trip we discovered on the morning of our conference that the road outside the hotel had been closed by the police for a major triathlon event as part of international tournament. Athletes had travelled from all over Africa to compete. However, I was scheduled to be the keynote speaker at the leaders conference that morning.

The organising Bishop and I prayed together and asked God for his favor to make a way where it seemed impossible. We then boldly requested the hotel security to ask the police to make an exception for us to travel. They approved as long as we left immediately. It was quite unusual driving down a road that was completely closed off with spectators expecting

INTRODUCTION

race competitors with other cars pulled over on the side of the road.

At a major intersection, a number of kilometres away, we were stopped by the police. We were told that we could not proceed and they were astounded that we had been allowed as far as we had travelled. We prayed again for favor. I boldly asked the policeman if he could make an exception for us given our circumstances. He asked his supervisor and to his surprise, the supervisor agreed for us to travel after the next bike rider passed. So we set off again passing many stationary cars, and other police checkpoints, until we were able to turn off to the conference venue.

All those who heard what had happened were astounded saying 'This never happens in Kenya!'

What had just happened? The favor of God had supernaturally broken into the impossible.

As well as providing protection, and access to greater levels of God's supernatural provision, did you know that the favor of God is meant to be part of your spiritual armour?
…..but more about that later!

Get ready to experience a whole new level of God's supernatural favor - Now!

CHAPTER 1

Why is Favor so Important?

Surely, Lord, you bless the righteous; you surround them with your FAVOR like a shield ...(Psalm 5:12)

Is Favor that important in the Bible?
Yes! It is 'front & center'!

Yet, I've discovered that when you start talking about the 'Favor of God' a lot of Christians look at you strangely. Well, it's because most Christians have never considered that the favor of God was something that they could experience on a daily basis.

Even more importantly, most do not realise that the 'Favor of God' is part of your warfare?

The truth is that not only is God's favor in the Bible, but it is also available to every believer – including you!

Jesus lived in the favor of God.

So can you!

We have God's favor with a wonderful prayer ministry in Jerusalem. The leaders have become like family. We try to go there each year to serve them and to help the house of prayer. Sometimes we stay up to 3 months at a time. However, 2025 was different as Israel was at war with Hamas. Even though rockets were still being fired into Israel, we sensed that God still wanted us to go to Jerusalem. God had given us the dates at the beginning of the year. This time we heard only to stay five weeks. So, we booked our flights for travel to Israel on 7th May and to return home on the 9th of June. Three days before we were due to fly to Israel on 4th May, a missile from Yemen hit Ben Gurien Airport in Tel Aviv. As a result, all international carriers stopped flying into Tel Aviv because it was too dangerous. However, we had a strong sense that God still wanted us to go. Every time we prayed we had His peace. When we checked our flights on the night we were due to depart, we discovered our airline, Emirates, was flying again. We obeyed God and decided to still go.

Emirates had resumed flights to Israel, using their affiliate, Fly Dubai, the very day we were scheduled to fly into Ben Gurion airport. No other airlines were operating. The arrival board had "Cancelled" against all other flights except ours. The favor of God had been released. [1]

It was a wonderful experience to land in Tel Aviv and see that we were the only aircraft at the international terminal (apart from a few Israel owned government flights). It was a strange but glorious experience to walk into a near empty Arrivals Hall. Instead of the normal crowds waiting at Border Control, there was only a handful of us, so we were able to enter easily.

Jerusalem was very quiet. There were very few tourists while we were there. The Old City was empty even though it was Pentecost season. The Messianic believers were so blessed that we had come to stand with them in faith. We were able to encourage and minister to many leaders while were there. We safely departed Israel on 9th June.

Three days later Iran fired missiles into Israel. Flights were cancelled again. This lasted for twelve days until the USA bombed Iran on 22nd June 2025. (2)

Because we had heard God's dates when to travel and had obeyed His directions we were safe once again. It was neither luck or coincidence. It was the supernatural favor of God.

We were perfectly protected and truly experienced the favor of God

'Surrounding us with His FAVOR like a shield'

as Psalm 5:12 declares.

The good news is that the favor of God is available to you as well to use as a shield.
You just need to know that the favor of God is part of your salvation and your inheritance as a son and daughter of Father God.

When my eldest daughter Rebecca was first married, my wife missed her more than she thought she would. After my daughter returned home from her honeymoon, I asked Rebecca to come to visit her mother. She was happy to do that. When she arrived, she opened the front door and called out 'Mom and Dad, I'm here'.

When she arrived, I thought she had gone to see her mother who was in our house of prayer. However, I heard a noise in the kitchen. I wondered who was there. I went out to discover my daughter with the door of our refrigerator open, eating her mother's cooking.

I was not surprised. In fact, I was very blessed for a very important reason!

Why? My daughter knew that what belonged to her father belonged to her.
I want you to understand the power of this story.

We also need to know that what belongs to God our Father also belongs to us!

This includes His supernatural favor!

Why is favor so important?

Jesus lived and taught that the favor of God was ours to live in and decree for others.

It was an essential part of His character and His destiny!

Where is that in the Bible?

The prophet Isaiah prophesied in Isaiah 61:1-2 about the coming messiah –

> *The Spirit of the Sovereign Lord is on me,*
> *because the Lord has anointed me*
> *to proclaim good news to the poor.*
> *He has sent me to bind up the broken hearted,*
> *to proclaim freedom for the captives*
> *and release from darkness for the prisoners,*
> *to proclaim the year of the Lord's "FAVOR"*

In Luke 4, we are told that Jesus entered the synagogue in Capernaum on the Sabbath. He reads that same scripture, Isaiah 61:1-2, out loud for all to hear …

Luke 4:20 tells us

> *Then he rolled up the scroll, gave it back to the attendant and sat down. The eyes of everyone in the synagogue were fastened on him.*

He then decrees in Luke 4:21

> *"Today this scripture is FULFILLED in your hearing."*

Jesus declares that He is the anointed Messiah. He is the fulfillment of that prophecy!

That was significant! For those present and all humankind until the end of time.

It is important to notice that Jesus ends with the verse…..

"To proclaim the Year of the Lord's FAVOR"

Jesus stops right there with the word FAVOR!

Now if you compare it with Isaiah 61:1-2, there is an additional phrase that Jesus did not read

"…The Day of Vengeance of our God.."

It is important to realize that Jesus has not only taken our sins, but he also took our judgement!

He replaced 'judgement' for our sins with 'Salvation & Favor".

Salvation and Favor

Paul the apostle taught how important it is for every believer to understand favor. He understood that 'favor' was (and still is) an essential part of the grace of God that we receive when we receive Christ's free gift of salvation!

When we receive His Grace, His unconditional love, His forgiveness and His freedom from the consequences of our sins, we also receive His favor!

He emphasised this truth when he taught the believers in church of Corinth.

In 2 Corinthians 6:1-2 Paul declares

> As God's co-workers we urge you not to receive God's grace in vain. For he says, "In THE TIME of my FAVOR I heard you, and in the day of salvation I helped you."

When you are born again, according to Ephesians 2:8 you receive this 'grace' and it is received 'through faith',

> 'It is the gift of God'

Even if Jesus is already your savour receive His free gift of 'Salvation and Favor' today.

It is important to emphasise your need for salvation in Christ Jesus. Jesus is the Way Truth and Life. There is no other way to God.

Paul decrees to us in 2 Corinthians 6:2 that NOW is the DAY of SALVATION.

If you have never asked Christ to take control of your life as your Lord and Savior - Good news - Today is the day of your salvation! Turn to Appendix 3 and pray that prayer and receive Jesus NOW.

2 Corinthians 6:2 also says that today...

NOW is also...

The TIME of God's FAVOR

CHAPTER 2

What does God's Favor Look Like?

To live in the favor, you first must understand it!

Favor Defined

Divine "favor" is God's grace, kindness, approval, and goodwill shown to us. [1]

As a result, we are freely given blessings, protection, and preferential treatment that is not earned by us.

Divine Favor

- Grace and Kindness:

God's favor is an expression of His grace and kindness towards us as His sons and daughters.

- Approval and Acceptance:

Favor is an overflow of God's love and acceptance, often

described as being "His beloved in whom He is well pleased".

- Blessings and Protection:

God's favor can be material blessings, spiritual gifts, protection, and overall well-being, surrounding a person "like a shield".

- Unmerited favor:

Divine favor can not be earned by you. It is a gift given to you by God. We don't deserve it. It is freely given by our Heavenly Father. It is God's unmerited grace.

The New Testament reveals that Jesus Christ embodies divine favor toward all of humankind.

Luke 2:52 says

> *Jesus grew in wisdom and stature, and in favor with God and man.*

Through Jesus Incarnation His favor becomes accessible to all who believe. Christ is our bridge between sinful humanity and a holy God. [2]

Personal Favor

- Goodwill and Approval:

This is the most common meaning of favor.

Favor can also describe the positive approval, or kindness that people show to each other.

- Preferential Treatment:

It can involve being given preferential treatment, leading to undeserved support and even promotion.

Other expressions of favor are:
- Attractiveness, beauty and charm so you stand out more than others
- When you're given a gift as a mark of kindness.

This has evolved into the common meaning of a small party favor.

The Favor of God is all these things and more.

It always fascinates me how our understanding of words that we use today differs greatly from their original meaning.

There are many biblical examples of this.
For example, the Holy Spirit being our 'comforter'.
The word 'comfort' does not mean a "poor me, warm fuzzy feeling".

The Middle Ages English meaning of the word 'comfort' means to be prodded; to strengthen; to step out boldly; be aggressively encouraged to do something that we wouldn't normally do."[3]

This is very different from what we understand today.

This is also the case with the biblical understanding of the word 'favor'.
When 'favor' was first used in the Bible, it was to do with salvation from a cataclysmic event because of God's judgement.

In the context of 2 Corinthians 6 it is important that we see salvation and favor again going hand in hand.

In Genesis 6:5-7 we are told that

> *The Lord saw how great the wickedness of the human race had become on the earth, and that every inclination of the thoughts of the human heart was only evil all the time.*
>
> *The Lord regretted that he had made human beings on the earth, and his heart was deeply troubled.*
>
> *So, the Lord said, "I will wipe from the face of the earth the human race I have created—and with them the animals, the birds and the creatures that move along the ground—for I regret that I have made them."*

Humankind was facing God's judgement because of their wickedness towards God and each other. So much so that He had decided to destroy all trace of the human race.

Except Noah!

Genesis 6:8 tells us that Noah

> *found FAVOR in God's eyes*

You might argue this is exactly the type of favor that you would have been looking for in that situation.

But God's favor is always for a divine reason and not just for your benefit.

Why did God choose Noah?

Genesis 6:9 says

> *Noah was a righteous man, blameless among the people of his time, and he walked faithfully with God.*

The God of Covenant had decided that He would begin the population of the world again.

So, God spares Noah, but it is for a divine purpose.
He instructs Noah to build Him an ark – a means to save mankind from themselves.

The reason why God chose Noah was because he was the only righteous man left.
He was uniquely qualified to populate the earth again!
This is also an amazing prophetic picture of us entering the favor of Christ's salvation in the new covenant that was to come.
Genesis 6:18 says

> *I will establish my covenant with you, and you will enter the ark—you and your sons and your wife and your sons' wives with you....*

Noah obeys God and builds the ark and he enters into it

> *two of all living creatures, male and female, to keep them alive.*

It is important to understand that the FAVOR of God was dependent on Noah's obedience to God's direction.

God's favor for us is also dependent on our response to God's specific direction to us.

Genesis 6:21 says

> *Noah did everything just as God commanded him.*

That is still the case for us all today.

Favor results in us being given unusual preference, approval and opportunity above others.

One of the best examples of this is Joseph being wrongfully accused yet receiving favor from the prison's warden.

Genesis 39:22-23 declares

> *But while Joseph was there in the prison, the Lord was with him; he showed him kindness and granted him favor in the eyes of the prison warden.*

> *So, the warden put Joseph in charge of all those held in the prison, and he was made responsible for all that was done there.*

The warden paid no attention to anything under Joseph's care, because the Lord was with Joseph and gave him success in whatever he did.

This is what favor looks like!

Sometimes, the favor of God is disguised in another form.

The best example of this is in Luke 1 when Mary has a visitation from the Arcangel Gabriel in the sixth month of her pregnancy.

It's hard to imagine how terrifying that would be. But it seems she was more concerned with Gabriel's greeting to her.

Gabriel tells her that she is favored twice!

First in Luke 1:28

> *"Greetings, you who are highly FAVORED! The Lord is with you."*

Mary wasn't so sure if she wanted this 'type' of favor.

Luke 1:29 tells us

> *Mary was greatly troubled at his words and wondered what kind of greeting this might be*

Then again in Luke 1:30, the angel said

> *Do not be afraid, Mary; YOU have found FAVOR with God*

The Angel goes on to say she will give birth to a son and call him Jesus.

Luke 1:34 says

> *How will this be," Mary asked the angel, "since I am a virgin?"*

She wasn't sure if this was the TYPE of FAVOR that she really wanted.

In Luke 1: 35-37 the angel answered

> *The Holy Spirit will come on you, and the power of the Most High will overshadow you. So, the holy one to be born will be called the Son of God.*
>
> *Even Elizabeth your relative is going to have a child in her old age, and she who was said to be unable to conceive is in her sixth month. For no word from God will ever fail."*

Mary makes the most amazing response to God's statement of favor, that the world has ever seen.

In Luke 1:38 she says

> *"I am the Lord's servant,"* Mary answered.
> *"May your word to me be fulfilled."*

What an incredible response from Mary to a declaration of God's favor to her!

That's why God the Father knew Mary was His chosen one to carry the saviour of the world in her womb.

As Bob Gass said [4]

> *If Catholics are guilty of making too much of Mary, we are guilty of not making enough of her.*

The old saying 'be careful of what you wish for' comes to mind. [5]

So many Christians desire the favor of God. But do you truly understand what you asking for?

It comes with incredible expectation and cost.

In Mary's case as an unwed teenage girl, God's 'favor" would come with potential rejection from her fiancé, condemnation, accusation, and even potential death because in the eyes of that culture would have presumed that she'd been promiscuous.

So much so that it took another angelic visitation to Joseph, Mary's fiancé, not to divorce her.

Matthew 1:18-24 tells us

> Mary was pledged to be married to Joseph, but before they came together, she was found to be pregnant through the Holy Spirit. Because Joseph her husband was faithful to the law and yet did not want to expose her to public disgrace, he had in mind to divorce her quietly. But after he had considered this, an angel of the Lord appeared to him in a dream and said, "Joseph, son of David, do not be afraid to take Mary home as your wife, because what is conceived in her is from the Holy Spirit. She will give birth to a son, and you are to give him the name Jesus, because he will save his people from their sins."
>
> All this took place to fulfill what the Lord had said through the prophet: "The virgin will conceive and give birth to a son, and they will call him Immanuel" (which means "God with us").

Verse 24 goes on to say

> When Joseph woke up, he did what the angel of the Lord had commanded him and took Mary home as his wife.

So, favor in the Bible looks very different to what we may have first understood.

The ultimate example of the favor of God in the Bible is Jesus.

In Luke 2 we are told that when Jesus was twelve years old, his parents Mary and Joseph took him up to Jerusalem for the Festival of Passover as they did every year. When all the Jews went up to Jerusalem they camped together in their tribe. Jesus and his parents belonged to the tribe of Judah. They always camped on the east side of the city of Jerusalem where the garden of Gethsemane is still located today. No wonder Jesus loved to go and pray there later an adult. He had lived and even played amongst the olive trees as a boy.

After Passover was over, because they were all travelling and staying within their large tribe Jesus parents began to return home. Without them realising it Jesus had stayed behind in Jerusalem.

Luke 2:44-45 says

Thinking he was in their company, they travelled on for a day.

Then they began looking for him among their relatives and friends.

When they did not find him, they went back to Jerusalem to look for him.

It took them three days to find him. They found him sitting in the courts of the temple courts, among the teachers, listening to them and asking them questions.

The scripture says that all those who heard him were 'amazed at his understanding and his answers'.

Verse 48 tells us

> When his parents saw him, they were astonished.
>
> His mother said to him, "Son, why have you treated us like this?
>
> Your father and I have been anxiously searching for you."

Jesus's answer was profound

> "Why were you searching for me?" ...
>
> "Didn't you know I had to be about my father's business?"

Then the Bible says something very significant in Luke 2:52

> Jesus grew in wisdom and stature, and IN FAVOR with God and man

This is so important for US too!
How do you grow in favor with God and people?

The answer is simple.

Jesus is the way to eternal life and FAVOR here on Earth.

Like Jesus we must always be careful to 'be about our heavenly Father's business here on earth'.

Decide today that you will follow hard after God the Father's purpose for your life.

Then you will grow in wisdom and stature, and IN FAVOR with God and man.

Decree: I have Salvation & Favor, not because of what I have done, but because of what Jesus has done for me.

Decree: Because of my obedience to God the Father, I grow in wisdom and stature, and IN FAVOR with God and man.

CHAPTER 3

Living in the Favor of God TODAY

If we are honest most of us do not live in God's Favor every day! However, this is not what God intends for us.

God the Father wants us to understand that as His children we can live in His favor. Many Christians may not be aware of what belongs to them in Christ.

It's like being left an inheritance without knowing about it.

Years ago, I read about a homeless man dying from extreme cold in the middle of winter on a street in the USA. Every death of someone is sad. What is the most sobering part of this story is that this man had inherited a fortune but wasn't aware of it.

A wealthy relative had left him their whole estate made up of houses and millions of dollars. The deceased relative's attorney had been looking for him for over 12 months to tell him what was legally his so he could begin to enjoy it.

However, it was too late for him. He lived his life without

realising what belonged to him.

God the Father does not want you to be like that person.

It is so important for you to understand that God wants you to live in favor today!

The Bible teaches that a principle is established by two or three witnesses.

First we see it in Deuteronomy 19:15

> *One witness shall not rise up against a man ... by the mouth of two or three witnesses shall a matter be established.*

Then in 2 Corinthians 13:1 Paul declares

> *In the mouth of two or three witnesses every word shall be established*

In biblical interpretation, when instruction appears more than once we need to take notice of that promise or direction.

It is not a surprise that the statement 'the time of God's favor' appears twice in the Bible.

Paul declares in 2 Corinthians 6:2

> *Now is the time of God's favor, now is the day of salvation*

Just before this Paul quotes Isaiah 49:8

> *This is what the Lord says:*
> *"In the time of my favor I will answer you,*
> *and in the day of salvation, I will help you*

Why?

Jesus fulfilled Isaiah's prophecy on the cross.

Because of what Jesus has done – that promise is for you and me NOW in our salvation in Christ!

Isaiah goes on in Isaiah 49:8 to prophesy what favor and salvation looks like for you – NOW!

Verse 8 says

> *I will keep you and make you to be a covenant people*

You are in HIS covenant family

> *to restore the land..*
> *to reassign desolate inheritances…*

God's Favor will restore lost generational inheritance.

Yes! You can go after in faith what has been lost by you and past generations and take it back in Jesus' name.

Isaiah 49:9 decrees

> *To say to the captives, 'Come out,'*
> *to those in darkness 'Be free!'*

Freedom from your sin and your past.

Freedom from all pain caused by the sin of others. Including your immediate family and past generations.

You are free today from those consequences in Jesus' name!

Decide to come out from underneath that now. Step into your freedom.

Isaiah 60:10(b) in the Passion Translation says it this way

> *I will restore you in my 'gracious' favor*
> *and show you my tender compassion.*

The Father wants to restore you in His gracious favor!

Favor is part of God's grace to us. 'Grace' is often explained as 'God's riches at Christ's expense'.

Part of God's riches for us is His favor.

He restores us graciously and tenderly.

Favor will even restore the consequences of your past mistakes.

I believe it is possible for you to go after any inheritance that you or previous generations have lost, even when you have sold property at the wrong time in the market.

God's favor will restore you. Either back to what was stolen from you or better than what you had before.

The key is to believe that God's favor will restore every part of your life.

You will experience favor of provision in the most unlikely ways and places.

In 1995 my non-Christian brother stood in disbelief on the block of land that my wife and I had just purchased.

We had only returned from overseas three years before with absolutely no money to plant a church.

He knew that we couldn't even afford the airfares for my wife and I and our five children to fly back to Australia. He also knew we had to borrow money to buy a car. My wife and I were only working part time because we were working full time for God.

He said to me *'Bruce how could you afford this?'*

I replied *'You're not going to like my answer... But it's the truth – God!'*

We not only bought the land, but we also built a family home.

There was no other explanation but the favor of God.

Isaiah 49:9 goes on to say you will

> *Find pasture on every barren hill*

Once you step into the favor of God you will experience supernatural provision that cannot be naturally explained.

Isaiah 49:10 decrees

> *They will neither hunger nor thirst*

The favor of God means that every need will be met even when your bank account says it's impossible.

We discovered very quickly when we started to live in the favor of God that it didn't matter what our bank balance said. God always provided. Every bill was always paid. There was always enough.

Isaiah 49:10

> *He who has compassion on them will guide them (us)*

The truth is it's never anything that we have done.
It's always because of His love for us, His sons and daughters.

Isaiah 49:10

> *and lead them besides springs of water*

One of the most wonderful things that the favor of God does is that it refreshes us. Not just because or when we receive supernatural provision but every day. When you are conscious of His favor and when you experience it even in a small way it refreshes you like a cool drink of water on a hot day.

The good news is that favor is like a spring. It never runs dry!

God's favor always supernaturally refreshes us by the power and presence of His Holy Spirit.

Verse 11 says

I will turn all my mountains into roads

The favor of God turns the greatest obstacles into miracles. They become testimonies of His love, faithfulness and power.

This is what God's favor is!

And it is yours NOW – TODAY!

Are you living in it?

Our Father is the giver of good gifts to us - His children.

Matthew 7:11

> *If you, then, though you are evil, know how to give good gifts to your children,* **how much more** *will your Father in heaven give good gifts to those who ask him!*

We don't have to beg or demand that He will do it.

The truth is that we are acting like orphans not sons.

I see so many Christians acting like the older brother in the parable of the prodigal son.

Jesus wanted to make sure that we understood this important truth.

It is why He finishes the parable with this powerful statement in Luke 15:31 –

> *'My son,' the father said, 'you are always with me, and everything I have is yours.*

He does not withhold it from you!

Expect it

We not only have to understand what the favor of God is we need to expect it each day.

I've learned to expect God's favor every day.

One of the ways to experience this is to step into it by faith on a daily basis.

Therefore, I make a number of decrees every morning.

The first is that;

> *Favor, favor, favor goes before me and surrounds me today!*

I have found that the more I speak it the more I believe it.

The more I believe it, the more I expect it to happen in my life that day.

Are we able to pray like that? Absolutely.

Remember, Psalm 5:12 declares;

> *Surely Lord, you will bless the righteous*
> *You surround them with your favor as with a shield*

If you know that you are righteous because of the blood of Jesus and you are living each day for Him, you can boldly declare that God will bless you and surround you with favor today and every day.

Favor is Dependant on Us

According to Scripture, favor is dependant on us!

Psalm 84:11 tells us that He freely gives us Favor and Honor.

> *The Lord bestows favor and honor*

> no good thing does He withhold
> from those whose walk is blameless

It is dependent on us.

Like Paul says about our salvation in Galatians 5:13

> You are called to be free. Do not use your freedom to indulge the flesh

In other words, we must live a godly life to
live in the blessing and favor of God. Blessing and favor always follows obedience to God.
The measure of His favor is dependent on us.
We must radically obey Him.
It is for those with the integrity of Joseph, the faith of Abraham and the obedience of Mary;

> For those whose walk is blameless

Once you have grabbed a hold of this and made it part of your life then you will learn to ...

Position yourself in His Favor

To live in the Favor of God you must position yourself IN it!

How do you do that?

You intentionally do it by faith every day.

Hebrews 11:1

> *NOW Faith is the SUBSTANCE...*
> *And... the EVIDENCE of things Not seen...*

'Substance' and 'evidence' are strong words.

The Greek word for 'Substance' in Hebrews 11 is *'hypostasis'* which means;

> *That which stands under* [1]

It is foundational.
Faith is the foundation for you to receive favor from God!

The Amplified version of Hebrews 11:1 says it this way

> *Now faith is the assurance (title deed, confirmation)*
> *of things hoped for (divinely guaranteed),*
> *and the evidence of things not seen [the conviction of*
> *their reality—faith comprehends as fact what cannot*
> *be experienced by the physical senses]*

Wow! When you exercise your faith to live in the favor of God, it becomes a daily reality in your life.
This is how to live in favor every day.

It works!

You just need to decide to 'work on your faith for favor' daily.

Favor Decrees

It's time to make some decrees-

Decree: The favor of God "Depends on Me"!

Decree: I am going to begin to live in favor from today!

Decree: I choose to position myself in God's Favor today and every day!

Decree: I expect God's Favor in my life!

Decree: Favor, Favor, Favor, goes before me and surrounds me like the shield today!

Decree: TODAY is the day of God's favor for my life!

Decree: Favor is NOW!

CHAPTER 4

Next Level Favor Operating System

There is a next level favor operating system available for you to step up into.

My wife Cheryl and I have now been in full time ministry for over forty years.

The longer we do this the more we realise how strategic we must be in transforming nations.

To do this you need to know how to use your spiritual weapons.

It is much more than knowing how to pray.

We also need to know how to fight spiritually and know how to dismantle assignments - Not just pray and fight against them.

There must be a shift in our mindset and prayer strategy from DEFENCE to OFFENCE.

Most Christians live in defence. This becomes obvious by the way a person speaks.

The favor of God is one of the best spiritual weapons.

You need to grow in your understanding of how to use the favor of God as a spiritual weapon.

The key is to know how to do that.

One key scripture is Psalm 5:12 -

> Surely, Lord, you bless the righteous; **you surround them with your favor as with a shield**

Psalm 5:12 in the Passion Translation powerfully says it this way:

> Lord, how wonderfully you bless the righteous.
> **Your favor wraps around each one and covers them**
> under your canopy of kindness and joy

Favor is one of the ways to overcome barriers and dismantle obstacles.

My family and I moved to the United States when I was a young assistant pastor in 1989. We moved there for me to study a master's degree in Church Growth and Leadership at Fuller Seminary in Pasadena, California. [1]

Our savings soon began to dwindle after nine months so I applied for a part time job at the Fuller Seminary Business Office. With my student visa I was allowed to work up to 20 hours a week.

It soon became obvious to us that I couldn't continue with my studies earning only a part time income. So, I was bold and asked the manager of the Fuller Business Office if they would sponsor me for a work visa so I could apply for a full-time job with them. One problem was that I was there only on a student visa. The challenge was that the USA would only allow a person to apply for a Working Visa in the United States before they entered the country. We were already living there.

God had another plan. His destiny reason for us moving to United States was to align with Che Ahn and Lou Engle whose church was in Pasadena.

Even though we weren't aware of this at that time, we still stepped out in faith and applied for a working visa in the USA while we were living there. We were told it was impossible.

However, God made a way where there was no way!

We received the supernatural favor of God! I was issued a working visa even though I was already in the country working for the organisation.

Favor went before us like a shield and cut through all the red tape and the impossible!

This was my first experience with the favor of God breaking through impossible barriers. Yes we had to fast and pray. Yes we had to exercise our faith.

Most importantly, we learnt a valuable lesson. Favor is not a one-off thing that happens sometimes to Christians.

It needs to be added to your warfare arsenal!

It is important to learn how to step into the favor of God as an act of warfare.

Develop a Stronghold Authority of Favor and Blessing

In 2 Chronicles 14, King Asa, the King of Judah

> He did what was right in the eyes of the Lord His God'

As we read in Psalm 5:12, when we live this life the favor of God comes on us. And it goes before us, and it gives us success and supernatural breakthrough. This is exactly what happened to King Asa.

However, he happened to realise that he just couldn't relax and no longer be on a war footing. He understood that the favor and blessing of God required for him to be always battle ready.

So as 2 Chronicles 14:7 says King Asa made a very strategic and powerful Godly decision.

> Let us BUILD UP these towns…and WALLS around them with TOWERS, GATES and BARS

Then he decrees-

> The Land is still Ours because we have sought the Lord our God – We sought Him and He has given us REST on every side…

2 Chronicles 14 goes on to say

> So, they BUILT and PROSPERED!

This is the result of supernatural favor warfare operating system.
It works.

Their Posture was a War Footing in the midst of peace

One of my favorite places in the whole of Israel is the City of

David in Jerusalem.

The City of David was David's palace or House of David.

You can have a guided tour through it today.

It's situated just outside of the walls of the Old city walls today. In King David's day it was inside the city walls of Jerusalem.

It was located very strategically.

2 Samuel 5:6-7 says

> King David and his men marched to Jerusalem to attack the Jebusites, who lived there. The Jebusites said to David, "You will not get in here; even the blind and the lame can ward you off." They thought, "David cannot get in here." Nevertheless, David captured the fortress of Zion—which is the City of David

David took up residence in the fortress and called it the City of David.

It is just outside the main Southern entrance steps that go up to the Temple Mount where Solomon later built the Temple of the Lord.

So David lived near to where the priests offered sacrifices of worship daily. David made sure that he was always close to the presence of God.

It overlooks the Kidron Valley. Jerusalem is a high place

set on the top of seven mountains. The track up the Kidron Valley was the entrance into Jerusalem. As Israel had many enemies, David knew he always had to be on a war footing. So he watched for them every day from his "fortress of the Lord".

David fortified his position and authority – so must we!

He reigned from the City of David with a heart of righteousness, resulting in the blessing and favor of God.

He not only lived in the 'Stronghold of the Lord', but He also BECAME a 'Stronghold of the Lord'.

We need to learn to LIVE in a Stronghold of the Lord too!

How did David do that?

In Psalm 18 David teaches us an amazing progression of spiritual authority –

>From Righteousness to Blessing.
>From Blessing to Favor.
>From Favor to Stronghold.

He declares in Psalm 18:2

> *I love you, Lord, my strength.*
> *The Lord is my rock, my fortress and my deliverer,*
> *my God is my rock in whom I take refuge, my shield*
> *and the horn of my salvation, my Stronghold.*

What is a Stronghold?

It is defined as-

> A place that has been FORTIFIED so as to protect it against attack / bondage [2]

When Christians use the word 'stronghold', it normally is being referred to in the negative. For example: - demonic strongholds.

However, there is another definition that is not negative. It is possible to have a 'positive' stronghold.

So, a positive meaning of 'Stronghold' for us is: -

> Place where a particular cause or belief is strongly defended.[3]

For example: - Your Godly mindset becomes a 'stronghold of the Lord's favor'.

It's time to fortify your favor position. You can become a 'Stronghold of the Lord'.

How do you step into and live in the 'Stronghold of faith-filled favor and authority'?

I picture myself each morning dressing myself in the armor of God. When I get to the shield of faith I see myself stepping into and being surrounded by the shield of faith filled with favor and blessing. I see myself entering and becoming the stronghold of the Lord. Like King David, I enter the stronghold and rule by faith, authority and power from a posture of righteousness, blessing and favor!

In Psalm 18, King David tells us in verse 25: -

> *To the faithful you show yourself faithful,*
> *To the blameless you show yourself blameless,*
> *To the pure you show yourself pure...*

Favor as a Weapon of our Warfare

Did you know that the 'Favor of God' is a weapon of spiritual warfare?

In fact, you can use the 'Favor of God' to push back the spiritual opposition that comes against you when you step out in obedience and faith on assignment for God.

Learn How to Dismantle Assignments

David goes on in verse 28 to teach us how to dismantle assignments against us:

> *You, Lord, keep my lamp burning; my God turns my darkness into light*

There is a way for you to learn how to dismantle assignments.

Because Jesus has given us power and Authority over all the power of the enemy, we can dismantle assignments when they come at us. I learned this in a practical way.

When there is criticism, false accusations, and even obstacles you can systematically take those assignments apart piece by piece.

I often imagine the arms and the legs of the assignment being taken apart and the mouth being sewn up. In the process you're able to bind the strongman Jesus teaches us in Matthew 18.

As a result, God turns 'your darkness into light'.

Victory and Advance

Then in verse 29 he says -

> With your help I can **advance** against a troop…with my God I can scale a wall

We need to have more than a battle mindset.

It is important to learn how to step into victory in your thinking, faith expectation, and words of faith.

I have discovered the more we think and speak faith in victory, our words become flesh. When we develop a victory mindset, and activate our faith by speaking the promises of God we learn how to advance.

We need to learn how to advance in faith and authority. As you will see, favor of God is part of this strategy.

This is the way to enter this next level of authority, breakthrough and favor operating system.

I learned this years ago when we were rezoning land for our church building. Our state government did not have a zoning allocation for church organisations. So, it was very difficult and most unusual for them to approve land being moved from residential purposes to a church use. Even though we had filled in all the required paperwork we still were having our application stalled. After prayer I decided that the Lord was leading me to go into the actual government office and speak to the employee responsible. I arrived to find a line-up of people. The person in charge was not having a good day and was being quite aggressive and rude. All those people before me were having their applications either denied or told their application was incorrect and they needed to go away and begin the process again. I remember quietly taking authority over the spirit of control that was operating through that government employee that day. The person immediately before me had their request turned down. Then it was my turn.

When the government employee spoke to me her countenance was completely different from everybody else she'd spoken to before me.

She simply smiled at me and respectfully said 'Yes Sir' then approved and stamped our rezoning application.

Thankfully I knew who I was in Christ and how to 'advance against' the opposition of control and 'scale a wall' of impossibility.

This is how the favor of God operates through us.

Faith Shields Up

It's important to always have your shield of faith and favor expectation up in front of you.

I recently heard an Australian leader speak about how she had just finished preaching a powerful message one day. A lot of people were converted to Christ, healed and helped by her ministry. As she went to collect her things at the end of the church service, someone came up to her and verbally attacked her. She was surprised as it was undeserved and unexpected.

When she prayed about the situation, she asked the Father 'What did I miss?'

She heard Him say – 'You didn't have your shield of faith up!'

Make sure your armor of God has a favor shield.

You need to step into the favor of God as a shield each day. My armor of God has a faith shield of favor. So does yours!

As Paul teaches us in Ephesians 6:10-17 put on the whole armor of God that includes the shield of faith.

Begin to use your Godly imagination as you spiritually dress yourself each day.

See the favor of God surrounding you like a shield of faith. Don't just see it around you, step into it and allow it to wrap around you.

Psalm 18:30 instructs us

As for God, his way is perfect: The Lord's word is flawless.
He SHIELDS ALL who take refuge in him

It is more than lifting a shield.
You must step into the shield and stronghold of the Lord!

We need to learn how to build and then maintain a 'fortress mindset'.
Not just in a time of warfare when we pray against opposition and obstacles.
We must keep building the fortress of faith, blessing and favor in the midst of peace.

Psalm 84:4-9 are important steps that every believer should

use as part of their spiritual warfare weaponry. Most of them you will have heard of before and hopefully use.

Verse 4 says

> *Blessed are those who dwell in your house, they are ever praising you.*

There is power in praise! It is part of your armor.

Other weapons include doing what verse 5 says 'setting your heart on pilgrimage' each day.

This means we keep the God vision in front of us, and we don't lose focus or give up no matter what. Learn how to learn how to pass through the Valley of Weeping and make your hardship a place of springs.

Then as verse 7 says we will then go

> *from strength to strength*

The overriding part of our armor shield is 'The Favor of God.'

Psalm 84:9 tells us that we should

> EXPECT God's FAVOR on you as His anointed ones

Yes – you need to make sure your armor each day has favor as a shield.

But do you know how to do that?
It is more than quoting 'favor' scriptures. That is a good start.

You need to believe that the power of the favor of God is working for you each day.

It is expecting the favor of God to go before you and fight for you as part of your impenetrable strength

How do you do this?

Learn How to Live in Impenetrable Strength

Psalm 18:32 tells us this way

> *It is God who arms me with strength and keeps my way secure*

You need to learn how to live IN the stronghold of the Lord each day.

It's like learning to drive a car. Initially you must think about the process and go through each step that's required for the car to move and stay in the right lane and get forward momentum. The more you practice the easier becomes and the more effective you are.

After a while it becomes second nature. You don't have to think any more, you automatically go through the right actions to get to your destination.

It is the same principle that you use to learn how to rise up in this new operating system of blessing and favor.

'The Favor of God' is more than a nice feeling or even an expectation.

I declare Psalm 90:17 over you today

> *The favor of God rests on you and establishes the work of your hands* (BL Paraphrase)

It is powerful, and forceful.
It will turn the most impossible situation around.
Even more, it will establish and bring the work of the Lord in reality.

Kingdom purpose will advance when the favor of God is activated as an act of war.

The good news is that this is not just for me and a select few! You can live like this in 'favor authority' from today on.

NEXT LEVEL FAVOR OPERATING SYSTEM

Decide to step up into this next level favor operating system right now!

CHAPTER 5

Blessed and Highly Favored

God wants to give favor to all of His children. Not just a few like Mary or King David.

The truth is that we all become His sons and daughters when we are born-again by His Holy Spirit!

When He looks at us – He sees us ALL as 'blessed and Highly favored!'

So, we are all His favorites. If we are His favorite, we can live in His favor every day.

How do we experience this?

Every child wants to know their father and mother!

God knows us intimately! And He wants us to know Him intimately.

Often people ask me if it is possible to know God this way? I always answer the same way - absolutely!

The Word of God confirms this in Psalm 139:10

You have searched me Lord and you know me. You know when I sit and when I rise. You perceive my thoughts from afar......"

David knew God this way. He goes on to say in verse 13

For you created my inner being you knit me together in my mother's womb..."

In verse 16 he says

Your eyes saw my unformed body; all the days are designed for me were written in your book before one of them came to be."

The apostle Paul prayed for us in Ephesians 1:17 that all believers would 'know God' this way. He prayed

I keep asking that the God of our Lord Jesus Christ the glorious Father may give you the spirit of wisdom and revelation so that you may know him better.

The truth is you can know someone by name and even be on speaking terms with them but not truly know them. In the West we often say we "know" somebody, but the truth is we don't know them at all. What does Paul mean when he talks about knowing God? Paul is saying that it is possible to have an intimate relationship with God. When someone told me that as young man I had trouble comprehending it. How could that be? The answer of course is through God's son Jesus Christ. He has made a way for you and me to go past all the ceremony and restrictions into a deep place of relationship, intimate relationship with God the Father.

True relationships are not one-way. If you are married to someone who only ever spoke to you when they were upset or in crisis and never stopped to listen to what you had to say, I can imagine you would say that that's not much of a marriage. Yet that best describes most people's relationship with God. When they pray, they only use a monologue without ever stopping to listen to what God has to say to them.

It is possible to have an intimate relationship with God the Father.

How intimate? The same type of intimacy as a husband and wife. Now I'm just not talking about a sexual intimacy. Often when my wife and I are with a large group of people in a party setting and we are in different parts of the room, when our eyes meet I can just make a facial expression, and she knows exactly what I'm thinking.

I can look at her in a certain way, and she nods in reply knowing immediately that it's time to go. Perhaps I raise my eyebrows in a certain way, and she will laugh even though no words are being spoken to each other.

Why? Because she knows exactly what I'm thinking. I think most couples who know each other well relate together this way. It is because we have spent time with each other building relationship. We know how to listen and to communicate with each other.

The basis of true relationship is always love. When you love someone you begin to know that person intimately.

1 Corinthians 8:3 says

If anyone loves God he is known by God.

So, to love God is to truly know Him.

God wants us to know His father's heart and to experience Him intimately.

Intimacy with God is essential. Without intimacy you will never truly discover your identity. Bill Johnson teaches that intimacy is also the basis of our authority. I've discovered that those with great spiritual authority always know who they are in Christ. Not only are they confident of their identity in Him but they also have an ongoing intimate relationship with God the Father.

If you don't have a personal relationship with God the Father, you may struggle to understand what true intimacy with God is.

The thing that changed most for me after I had that encounter with the Father heart of God in Mozambique in 2008, was my prayer life. (1)

I am a light sleeper so I'm often awake during the night. Before encountering the 'Father heart' of God I would lay awake worrying or thinking so much that I couldn't go back to sleep.

Now if I wake I have learnt just to lean into my heavenly Father.

I step straight into intimacy with the words "I love you Daddy God" and immediately I hear him say back "I love you too son". His presence always comes in that instant. I sense His amazing, and unconditional love. Often I'm caught up for long periods of time in his presence. The fruit of these times are always amazing. However, such a great sense of being His son and knowing exactly how He wants me to live and what He wants me to do.

Intimacy with God the Father is so important. There is nothing you can do that will ever separate you from His love.

Romans 8:38-39 says

> *And I am convinced that nothing can ever separate us from God's love. Neither death nor life, neither angels nor demons, neither our fears for today nor our worries about tomorrow—not even the powers of*

hell can separate us from God's love. No power in the sky above or in the earth below—indeed, **nothing in all creation will ever be able to separate us from the love of God** that is revealed in Christ Jesus our Lord
(NLT)

The Father has Lavished His Blessing and Favor on you!

Your Father not only loves you, but He also delights in lavishing His love on you.

'Lavish' is not a word we use often today but it is a powerful and beautiful word.

John the apostle, was known as the apostle of love. Folklore says that whenever he got up to speak, he would begin and end with "love one another".

In 1 John 3:1 it says

"…. what great love the father has LAVISHED on us"

To 'lavish' means to
"expend or give in great amounts; without limit; to bestow in abundance or shower."

The great news is that the Lord lavishes His love, blessing and favor on you!

This means that there is no limit to the love, blessing and favor the Father lavishes on you today. When we are given a birthday present that is gift wrapped you only receive it after you have unwrapped it.

One Christmas, I received more gifts than usual. Due to the large volume of gift paper, I overlooked unwrapping one of my smaller gifts. It was only discovered a few days later.

I sensed the Holy Spirit teaching me the gift is only received when it is unwrapped.

This amazing blessing and favor has been given to us. Yet we must receive it. We must unwrap it in our lives before it will become a reality in us.

He wants to lavish it on us. It seems back to front. He is the worthy One! He should be having all the love lavished on Him! But He has lavished it on us.

Why does He do this?

So, we can become the children of God.

Now you might be saying as you read this 'Yes, ... I know I

am God's child!' But do you truly know the love that practically transforms you from being an orphan to an adopted son or daughter?

In Romans 8:14-15, the Greek word for *adoption to sonship* is a legal term referring to the full legal standing of an adopted male heir in Roman culture. It was a big deal to be a Roman citizen and even bigger deal to be the male heir.

The English word "adoption" is not the best translation for this term.

The more correct translation is the 'spirit of sonship.'

You see when you received the 'spirit of sonship' your DNA changes so that you receive the same DNA as your father. This is not the same for an orphan who is adopted. When you are adopted, you might change your name to your father's name, but you still have your birth mother and father's DNA.

When you receive the 'spirit of sonship' you are more than adopted, you are so loved by the Father that you become like Him in every way.

I love seeing older married couples who have been married for decades and are obviously still in love. They have loved each other so strongly that their physical appearance changes and they end up looking like each other. When you receive the 'spirit of sonship' and allow the Father to lavish His love on you, you begin to become like Him! You reflect His love to others wherever you go.

It gets even better.

How do we become Loved, Blessed and Highly Favored?

When you receive the 'spirit of sonship' you become His child!
Your relationship with God moves.

It moves from trying to please those who act as father figures.

It moves from serving God out of expectation to willingness.

It moves from serving Him out of obligation to joy.

It moves from pleasing Him out of fear to freedom.

Paul says *The spirit you received does not make you slaves so that you live in fear again.*

You are able to move from fear to sonship.
To knowing that He loves you as His son and daughter to be your Abba Father!

God the Father doesn't want you to please Him, or to serve Him out of obligation because you are afraid of Him or because it's expected.

Paul says it this way in Galatians 4:4-7

> But when the <u>set time</u> had fully come, God sent his Son, born of a woman, born under the law, to redeem those under the law, that we might <u>receive adoption to sonship</u>. Because you are his sons, God sent the Spirit of his Son into our hearts, the Spirit who calls out, "Abba, Father."

Paul tells us at the 'set time' God sent His Son. Now is your 'set time'.

By His 'spirit of sonship', you are now able to live as His son or daughter!

Something in your DNA has changed!

You are not an orphan! But a son or a daughter!

The first thing that happens is that you have immediate intimacy with God the Father.

It is immediate because you instantly sense His overwhelming acceptance and limitless love.

You sense His amazing presence in your heart instantly.

When you tell Him that you love Him you hear Him telling you how much He loves you.

You can hear His voice more clearly than you ever could previously.

It is a heart-to-heart connection that compares to nothing else you can ever experience. His deep limitless love instantly is revealed into your heart.

You become His beloved son, His beloved daughter.
So much so when read Luke 3:22 it is not presumptuous to superimpose your name in place of the Son of God!!

He says over you today,

> *You are my son/daughter, whom I love; with whom I am well pleased*

Your Sonship is that powerful! It is that real! It is that WONDERFUL.

The good news is that if you are a son or a daughter, then you are also an heir!

Galatians 4:7 says

> *So, you are ... God's child; and since you are his child, God has made you also an heir*

Occasionally in the media there are court cases where the children of a deceased millionaire are contesting the will because they were not included in the inheritance. It would appear they would have no right to their father's estate because they were not specifically mentioned in his will as inheriting anything. Most times they receive a ruling in their favor.

Why? Because they are the son or daughter and they have their father's DNA, so they have a right to be an heir! They want what belongs to them – their inheritance!

The good news is you are not just any son or daughter.

You are sons and daughters of Abba Father! The Father of all fathers! The God of all gods!

When you are born-again of incorruptible seed you have been transformed by the 'spirit of sonship'.

What is your inheritance?

Whatever belongs to God the Father belongs to you. This is why God's favor is yours every day.

You are LOVED
You are BLESSED
You are HIGHLY FAVORED

Why don't you declare it right now!

Decree-

"I am His precious son / daughter whom He loves and with whom He is well pleased!"

As you decree that powerful revelation, I sense Him declaring over you……
'You are MY precious Son/Daughter.'
'You are MY Son/Daughter whom I love.'
'You are Blessed and Highly Favored.'

Something wonderful happens inside you when you get this revelation. Deep in your heart you begin to truly believe that
'I am HIS son/ HIS daughter.'
'I am Blessed and Highly Favored.'

Allow this to sink deeply into your soul!
Allow Him to reveal to you who you really are!

You are HIS SON…. HIS PRECIOUS SON
You are HIS DAUGHTER…. HIS PRECIOUS DAUGHTER
You are LOVED
You are BLESSED
YOU are HIGHLY FAVORED

CHAPTER 6

Blessing and Favor in the Spacious Place

Normally we do not associate 'blessing and favor' with hardship.

The good news is that even when we're facing tough times, God always has a way through your circumstances and every obstacle that you will face.

It gets even better than that.

The Increase of Blessing and Favor

Even though it may be hard to see at the time, when we respond God's way, blessing and favor increases in our lives through the hardship and challenge.

David is the best example of this.

When he was running for his life from King Saul, David encountered God in such a way that it transformed his life.

He will do the same for you.

In Psalm 31 we read that David was under acute pressure and facing death.

Amid all this pain, he had a revelation from God that he was increasing and growing in his pain.

In Psalm 31:8 David says something very profound for you and me-

You have set my feet in a spacious place.

The word 'spacious' is normally used to describe an open space or a large dwelling place.

But there is an even more specific definition;

Larger in extent or capacity than the average...

What does a 'spacious place' look like?

My wife Cheryl often talks about needing to go out of the city into the country or to the beach, so she has room to breathe - but that's not what a true spacious place is.

A spacious place is not a geographical change or a physical

place.

It is a place of deep encounter with God that transforms us and overflows into our future.

You thrive when this takes place. When you thrive you are healthy and strong, you will always do well, flourish and increase.

It always results in favor and blessing.

To live in a spacious place is more than a positive perspective and an optimistic outlook on life.

It means that you can live a life of passionate favor and blessing.

When you're in a spacious place you are blessed.

The Bible teaches us that we are made up of three parts - body, soul and spirit.

It is in your spirit that Jesus lives and where your conscience dwells. It is also where growth and maturity come from. You are grounded and at peace regardless of what is taking place in your life.

When you live this way, you are content, patient, grateful and blessed.

You have an inner peace which overflows onto others.

When David declared that God had set him in a spacious place, he was saying that God had blessed him with a greater capacity to cope and conquer in the most difficult circumstance. He understood what true blessing looked like.

We all have hardship. Sometimes it doesn't just last a short time! Saul was pursuing and attempting to kill David for many years. Despite all the fear and stress David stepped into a spacious place in God.

How to live in a spacious place

How do you live in a spacious place of favor?

Psalm 84:4 gives us the answer-

> *Blessed are those who dwell in your house, they are ever praising you.*
> *Blessed are those whose strength is in you, whose hearts are set on pilgrimage.*

We don't use the word pilgrimage much in western society these days.

Our ministry is connected to a House of Prayer in Jerusalem. We take teams on prayer assignments there each year.

We have learned that the easiest way to pass through passport control and border security in Tel Aviv is to say that we are entering Israel on 'pilgrimage'.

Pilgrims have been going to Israel for over 2000 years. But what is the true meaning of the word pilgrimage?

A 'pilgrimage' is best defined as-

> A person's journey through life, including personal growth.
>
> It involves a spiritual focus or pathway which leads you to an encounter with God". [1]

Normally we don't expect favor, blessing or growing closer to Jesus, to involve acute hardship.

Blessing in the wilderness

In Mark 1:9-11 Jesus had a wonderful experience at His baptism.

Heaven opened and the Holy Spirit fell on Him. He heard the Father tell Him that He was His beloved son. He would have felt very blessed.

But look at what happens next!

Mark 1:12 says-

> *At once the Spirit sent him out into the wilderness....*

What just happened?

God had just blessed Him remarkably but why did He have to go into the wilderness?

We have a problem with our western secular thinking. We don't equate 'blessing' and 'favor' with 'wilderness' experiences.

Wilderness was part of God's will for Jesus. And it will often be His will for us.

He wasn't just there for a few days. He was there for forty days. He wasn't camping and singing songs of worship around a campfire.

No! He was being tempted by Satan for forty days.

I remember when I broke my left hand and then a few months later I also broke my left shoulder. This was after surgery on that same shoulder three months before.

If you didn't know that Jesus had been led by God into the wilderness to be tempted by Satan and overcame it with power, and I told you that God had blessed me over those months, most would say 'that doesn't sound like God to me'.

Why? Because so many have no grid reference for it!

But the wilderness is where Jesus grew in great power. It was where He experienced the overflow of power, blessing and increase in favor.

In Luke 4:13-14 it says;

> When the devil had finished all this tempting, he left him ....
>
> And
> Jesus returned to Galilee in the power of the Spirit....

How did that happen?

The answer is what David discovered in Psalm 84:6. It says David learnt to

> .... **pass through** the valley of Baca.

The valley of Baca was well known in David's days. It literally meant 'the place of weeping'.

A place of weeping is a place of hardship and requires great endurance.
Most Christians would say, 'I never want to visit there...'

But you're missing the point!
You 'pass through' the valley of weeping. You don't live there!

David not only caught this truth, but he also lived it.

That's why he said in Psalm 23:4 NKJV and he decrees

> *even though I walk through the valley of the shadow of death...*

David understood that you are only meant to pass through hardship and pain including the valley of death, but you were never meant to live there!

It is the place of transformation.

The Blessing of Springs

If you're able to embrace this process, then something important happens when you are there.

You learn to do what David did in Psalm 84:6.
You will make your hardship and pain-

> *...a place of springs*

How do you make a place of hardship a place of springs?
The simple answer is you press into God when everything goes wrong. You don't run away from Him. You run to Him.

Here's some practical ideas that will help transform your valley of weeping into a place of springs and blessing.

- Worship. Have worship playing in your home. In the process you learn to truly rejoice in the Lord.
- Speaking in tongues increasingly every day.
- Encourage yourself in the word of God.
- Declare the promises of 'favor and blessing' out loud each day.

And make sure that you…Decree that -

The favor of God is on me today

I am blessed

I live in increased favor, and it overflows

I am surrounded by the favor of God and full of his blessing

When you do these things, you will turn your challenges into springs of the Blessing and Favor of God.

Springs are where living water flows!
This is what it means to live the victorious Christian life.
This is what it means to live in a spacious place.
You turn hardship into a place of springs, a place of encounter with God, a place of breakthrough blessing and favor.

So regardless of your present situation - how difficult or easy, how challenging or restful life maybe right now, God wants you to live in a spacious place.

Once we say 'Yes' to this lifestyle of living in a spacious place, God fills you with the power of His Holy Spirit to break through into a whole new way of living and increase.

The Favor of Strength

Many years ago, during a time of prayer I decided that I was never going to retire.

I heard the Lord say,

> Do not retire, instead refire.

I knew exactly what the Lord meant. He was telling me that ministry is a lifelong calling.

And if I said 'Yes' to that call, then He would give me longevity. And He would increase blessing and favor in my life.

So, every time somebody asks me when I'm going to retire, I always say-

> I am not retiring. I am refiring.

There is no retirement age to your call of God. You are not subject to a denomination or a church board or other people's opinions. You can keep going as long as God gives you strength.

In Deuteronomy 33 Moses decrees in verse 25 (NKJV)

As your days, so shall your strength be.

God's Word has many layers of context.

When God gave His people a promise in the Bible, we can expect that same promise as His son or daughter today.

When God promised long life to Asher, He was also promising the same to you!

The Longevity of Favor

We can also receive the longevity of favor.

It is not just a promise to live a long time. Now it's more than that!

The promise of longevity of years is also longevity of favor and blessing all the days of your life.

The context is that earlier in Deuteronomy 32, Moses was giving his final blessing to Israel before his death. He blesses each of the twelve tribes, one at a time.

Over each one he decreed their strength and prophesied their future.

In Deuteronomy 33:24 Moses blesses Asher.

He decrees-

Asher is the most blessed of all sons.

He goes on to decree –

Let Him be FAVORED by His brothers

Then he gives the powerful analogy-

Let him DIP his foot in OIL.

In other words, 'Let Asher be anointed for his future'.

In verse 25 NKJV he goes on-

The bolts of your GATES shall be iron & bronze.

Other Bible versions replace the word 'gates' with 'shoes.'

What was Moses saying?

He was saying to Asher that God will give him favor, strength, maturity, authority, and influence to walk in every day of his life.

God will do the same for you too!

This is what Blessing and Favor looks like.

The older I become the more I understand the power of this promise.

God has always intended that His sons and daughters live their whole lives in favor, blessing.

Not to limp or fall over the finish line. But to finish our race running with favor, blessing and power.

This promise of - '*As your days are so your strength will be*', is what blessing and favor looks like.

It is your choice.

Do you want longevity of favor and blessing in your life?

God's promise is true, and it is yours. Believe and receive it and it will become your reality. The promise is also for you to live all your life healthy and strong.

This is a great promise of 'long blessed and favor filled life'.

You will be favored and blessed all the days of your life.

Is this possible? Absolutely!

Decide, regardless of what obstacles you face in life, that you are going to increase in blessing and favor by choosing to live in a 'spacious place'.

CHAPTER 7

The Time is Now

The Time is Now!

It is Time.

What Time? God's 'Kairos Time'.[1]

In Galatians 4:4 (NKJV) Paul decrees

> When the 'set time' has fully come God sent for his son

'Set time' is also translated as

> When the 'fullness of time' had fully come

To have fullness of time means that, everything that God has ordained and required has been fulfilled.

The Jews were looking, longing that the Messiah would come.

The Romans were ruling Israel. They were prisoners in their own land. They were looking for the Messiah to come and deliver them.

But the Old Testament prophets like Isaiah and Daniel had prophesied His coming for generations.

At the time of Christ's birth, the people of that time were prepared for His coming. It truly was the 'fullness of time'.

'Set time' is the God ordained time.

When Jesus declared on the cross of Calvary *'It is finished'* it was and will always be redemption time for the whole of the human race.

This is fulfilment of time for every believer until Jesus returns to earth as Lord and King.

From then on...
It is and always will be Salvation time.
It is and always will be the Time of His Favor.

Important to SEE what time it is

Seeing the time is important.

I am a light sleeper and often I wake up in the middle of the night.

So having a smart watch beside my bed makes it easy for me to see what time it is.

I know it is God waking me up to pray when the time is either 1:11, 2:22, 3:33 or 4:44.

This is happening more than usual now.

Why? It is important to SEE what time it is.

We need to see what time it is NOW

James Goll is a remarkable prophet. When God first restored the office of the prophet to the body of Christ in the 1980s, James, as part of the Kansas City Prophets, was one of the forerunners God used to demonstrate that the time for office of the prophet was for today - NOW.

In 2008, we met James at the annual gathering of our international apostolic network - Harvest International Ministries in Pasadena California.[2]

We were then able to host him for his first visit to Australia in 2009.

He ministered in Australia throughout many cities and was very tired because of jet lag. After speaking at a morning session at the conference, he returned to his hotel to rest before he spoke at the afternoon session.

When I went to his hotel to pick him up for that session he did not respond when I knocked on his door. Apparently he was in a deep sleep.

So, I called out to wake him up.

James woke up and yelled out –

> *"What time is it?"*

Prophets are amazing. They hear what God is saying in the most unique way.

James knew that his statement *"What time is it?"* was more than just him waking up from a deep sleep.

He knew God was speaking to the body of Christ.

For the remaining time in Australia, James spoke on 'our need-to-know what time it is!'.

Discerning the timing of what God is doing he says is just as important as knowing what God is saying.

In 1 Chronicles 12:32, we are told that sons of Issachar were men who were able to

> *Discern the times*

Isaiah understood what God was doing, and he saw the timing.

He prophesied in Isaiah 22:19

> *See I am doing a new thing!*

We need to be able to see what God is doing and what time it is too.

Timing is Everything

Yes - Timing is everything!

After forty plus years of ministry I've noticed two things common to today's Christians:

First - Most don't know God's destiny for their life.

How do I know that? They are unable to clearly articulate their divine purpose.

I was so concerned about this that I wrote my first book – *Fathering a Destiny* – to help all Christians discover and step into their God destiny.[3]

Second - If they do know God's will, they often get the timing wrong.

They often step into it prematurely. They are in God's will but at the wrong time.

Why? They haven't learned to wait until they are sure they

have heard that that is God's timing.

Timing and obedience go together. It is important to get the right time.

God's Kairos time is God's *"right time"* or a *"set time"*.

It will always be confirmed as 'the most significant timing'. When you experience it you know that it is perfect timing. It is the right moment of opportunity, spiritual insight or significant decision.
This is how the favor of God works. And why prayer and obedience is so important.

My wife and I had our children close together, we were young in ministry, so our lives were very busy. We were juggling our role as assistant ministers in our growing church and our growing family. We lived across the road from the church which was both convenient and challenging.

Just before our fourth child, Sarah, was born, I was hosting a visiting speaker one night. I looked up to see my father-in-law entering the church in a hurry. I could tell he had come to tell me something important. Even though my wife was not due for a few more days, He came up to me and said -

The baby is coming, you need to come now.

My wife was in labour, and our baby was ready to come into

the world. It was her time to be born.

What time is it? It is NOW time

My wife is a prophet of prayer. In 2013 we had a House of Prayer in our home.

One day as we were finishing our prayer time, I was walking out the door and suddenly stopped. It was like someone hit me in the stomach. One moment I was walking and the next moment I was stopped in my tracks.

I turned to my wife and said -

> *"Something has just shifted!"*

Something had shifted in our nation...

I heard the Lord say

> *The old has gone the new has come*

That night, 24th August 2018, the prime minister of our nation was replaced by a new leader. He was the answer to months of strategic prayer asking God for a Christian godly leader for Australia.

In Australia we have a parliamentary system of government where the politicians elected vote to decide who will become prime minister. That night the existing prime minister was voted out, and a new prime minister was appointed.

Our new prime minister was not only a practicing Christian, but he was also a godly leader that believed that our nation needed Jesus as the answer.

It happened suddenly!

It was a time of dramatic change for Australia.

Isaiah the Prophet saw the need for dramatic change in Israel too!
He saw what was needed in his day, but he also looked into the future and saw it today too!

It is what God is doing right across the world in the body of Christ right now as well!
Like Isaiah, we have to see it for ourselves and look into the future for those who are still to come.

Do you perceive this?
Can you see it?
It has happened for everyone who believed since the time of Christ's death and resurrection.

It was since then...
And - It is happening right NOW!

But you have to see it.

Isaiah 43:19 goes on to say

> *NOW it springs up do you not perceive it!*

When does it spring up? NOW!

We have stopped saying revival is coming. If you can 'see' with His eyes you will see that it is already here. It is already here! If you can't see it, it means you are not looking with God's eyes!

We need to begin to SEE with GOD'S EYES!

"Now it springs up do you not PERCEIVE it…"

If you do not perceive or see what is happening spiritually, it is possible that you can have revival happening all around you and miss it!

There are so many examples of people praying for revival and missing it because it came in a way that they did not expect or perceive it would come.

The Asuza Street Pentecostal revival in 1906 is the classic example. There were a group of leaders in Los Angeles who were praying and believing for the same manifestation of revival that was taking place in Wales known as the Welsh

Revival. They wanted the same revival outpouring to come to Los Angeles, but their prayers were answered in a way that they did not expect.

Instead, God sent an African American from Oklahoma whose name was William Seymour to Los Angeles. He preached a passionate revival message that included a teaching many did not like - the baptism of the Holy Spirit accompanied by speaking in tongues.

But those who had been praying for revival could not "see" or "perceive" that this was God's answer to their prayers. They locked him out of the church when he returned to speak as scheduled that night. The very thing that they had been praying for they rejected because it didn't come packaged in the way they expected. They were bound by traditional perception or seeing, expectations and their past experience and could not perceive it spiritually.

Just because God moved in a certain way in your life in the past does not mean He will work that way in the future!

I want to challenge you to be willing to change your perception.

Decree with me: -

"I PERCEIVE what time it is – I SEE it."

God's Time is Now

My wife Cheryl has written a remarkable book *'An Army Arising to Shift the Nation'* to mobilise believers to rise up together in prayer and authority to shift nations into the kingdom of God. It is a strategic manual based on national transformation in over 5 nations.[4]

In it she released an important prophetic word:

> *I believe we are coming into a time of convergence. The right conditions for great change are appearing together. The culture, the technology, current mindsets and hardships are bringing people to the right place at the right time. The earth is poised, ready to receive the advance of the Kingdom of God. The army of God must rise and take this opportunity to bring in the great harvest of the nations. I believe God had bought us to an opportune time, a 'Kairos time' in the Kingdom.*

Cheryl goes on to share-

> *God brings his people and the world into convergence so that he can orchestrate opportune times for deliverance. When God bought the children of Israel out of Egypt after 430 years. It was an opportune time.*

It was in God's timing in history, when God bought all the necessary factors together to set His people free. I believe God has brought us, like the Israelites to the edge of the promised land and He is encouraging his people again to arise and possess their inheritance.

It is that time now.

This is the set time.

Now! Now! Now!

Now is the Day of Salvation!

Now is the Day of His Favor!

CHAPTER 8

Expecting the Favor of God Every Day

Expect God's favor today! I encourage you to expect the Favor of God every day.

As a young pastor, I read Jerry Savelle's book 'Walking in Divine Favor'.[1]

It was the first time I had heard anyone teach of how to live in God's favor.

He taught that-

> God's favor is a divine advantage that believers can activate through faith, obedience, and righteousness, leading to opportunities, open doors, and provision.

He would regularly ask

> What is your favor of God status today?

I learnt that the answer to the question should be the same every day – "I expect the favor of God to surround me and go before me today".

Walking Daily in the Promise and Abundance of Divine Favor

From the beginning of creation, God's favor is an unchanging gift to everyone who lives in relationship with Father — available, abundant, and personal. Remind yourself, this promise is not reserved for a select few, but for every believer in Jesus who is willing to trust, receive, and walk in His goodness.

That is, you!

God's favor is more than a pleasant experience; it is a vital spiritual reality.

Favor brings blessing, life, protection, guidance, and supernatural increase to you today and every day.

As Proverbs 8:35 declares,

> For those who find me find life and receive favor from the Lord.

This favor is the difference between striving in our own

strength and flourishing by God's grace today. Favor opens doors that you cannot open. It places us right in the centre of God's purpose, where His presence goes before us and prepares the way.

Expect it! Live in it!

God's favor will manifest in your life from the moment you are born again.

The early church experienced this daily. In the Book of Acts they shared everything.

In Acts 2:47

> *They enjoyed the favor of all the people. And the Lord added to their number daily those who were being saved.*

You can expect a remarkable turnaround in your circumstances, unexpected opportunities, answered prayers, to peace amid challenges and restoration after loss. This is what supernatural favor will do for you today and every day.

Favor looks like divine connections, protection in adversity, wisdom in decision-making, and joy that remains even when circumstances shift today.

The Favor of God is not coincidence, good fortune or luck.

Because of God's kindness, His favor is available to all believers who choose to live by faith.

The message encourages believers to expect and walk in God's favor continuously

Live in the Favor of God TODAY

Remember to declare every morning –

Favor is available to me today!

Living in God's favor is not a distant hope; it is a present reality for every believer.

Today, choose to align your expectations, words, and actions with the truth that you are favored by God.

Living in favor is not hard. The key is to live in daily relationship and obedience to Him. We have a role in living in the favor of God.

That is why James 4:6 reminds us that

God opposes the proud but shows favor to the humble

Humility and obedience will unlock the favor of God in your

life each day. When you walk in faith, gratitude, and obedience, you invite the fullness of God's blessing into your everyday life.

As you grow in understanding, you take your faith to the next level. Develop a daily "operating system" of expectancy, prayer, and gratitude. Speak favor over your family, work, and community.

Remember God wants to lead you into His "spacious place" — a realm of overflow, freedom, and abundance.

As Psalm 106:4 declares

> *Remember me, Lord, when you show favor to your people, come to my aid when you save them*

The spacious place is where blessing and favor meet and where limitations are left behind. Here, you are released into purpose, equipped for impact, and invited to live in God's abundance.

Step out boldly today, knowing God's goodness surrounds you.

Let each day be marked by an awareness that favor is not random — it is intentional, promised, and accessible. Move from simply hoping to confidently expecting His favor today.

Your identity as His child, means you are blessed and highly favored. The world may offer fleeting recognition, but God's favor establishes you, affirms you, and brings lasting joy today and every day.

Decree it with conviction:
> *I am blessed and highly favored today!*

You have Favor?

Remember that God's Favor is best defined as-
> A source of open doors: God's favor is seen as the force that "opens doors that no one can shut" and creates opportunities that would otherwise be inaccessible.

Anchored in Scripture

Let these scriptures anchor your heart and your expectation of His Favor today:

> *Proverbs 8:35: For those who find me find life and RECEIVE FAVOR from the Lord*

It is a way of life where God gives you a 'supernatural advantage, which is an unmerited, divine boost that goes beyond natural talent or effort.[2]

> Psalm 5:12: *You bless the righteous; you surround them with your FAVOR as a shield*

The Favor of God is a weapon of spiritual warfare. If you learn to see it that way, it will change the way you live as a believer.

God will wrap His favor around us which acts as a shield in times of challenge and even conflict.[3]

> 2 Corinthians 6:2: *Now is the time of God's FAVOR*

Choose to believe that your life of favor is real and continuous. Every morning, declare:

> *"I expect God's favor NOW."*

God's Favor is for others

Most importantly the favor of God is not only about you! Remember God's favor on your life is for others!

Favor is always about you giving His love to others.
It is always about Jesus.

Like Jesus as a boy in Luke 2:49 you must always

be about the father's business

The Favor of God in your life is Always about the Father and pointing others to JESUS

It must be the main reason why you expect the Favor of God each day.

Favor Arise

Expect the Favor of God to arise in you today.

His love and His grace is with you, and His favor surrounds you!

Step forward with faith, boldness, and joy, knowing the best is yet to come.

You are blessed, you are favored, and you are called to live in the Favor of God— every single day.

Favor is yours today!

Expect it!

Favor is yours!

Live in it!

CONCLUSION

My Final Favor Words for You

Well done! What an exciting journey of favor you are on.

As you step more into the favor of God you will become more aware of His favor in your life each day. His favor will be more evident than ever before.

Choose to align your expectations, words, and actions with the truth that you are favored by God.

I pray that every day you will see an increase of His favor working in your life. His favor is going before you. Even protecting you from decisions you will later realise would not have been best for you and your future.

You will discover favor scriptures that you haven't noticed before. People whom you don't even know will unexpectedly give you favor. You will have unexpected opportunities that you don't naturally deserve.

You will recognise that it is not by your ability, but God's supernatural blessing and grace that is giving favor to you.

David practised living this way when he was a young shepherd boy. Well before imagining that he would ever become the King of Israel he realizes all that God had blessed Him with. In Psalm 103:1-4 he declares the favor and benefits he was living in – forgiveness of all his sins, healing of all his diseases, redemption from discouragement and despair, crowning him with love and compassion and satisfying his desires with good things.

The good news is that 'God does not show favoritism' with His favor.[1]
He will do the same for you too!

And better still – because of Jesus' free gift of salvation it is available for all humankind.

In 2 Corinthians 6:2, God declares over you

> NOW is The TIME of God's FAVOR

Favor is yours NOW!

TODAY and EVERY DAY

Wow! Why wouldn't you want to live in His favor every day?

MY FINAL FAVOR WORDS FOR YOU

Here are some final decrees that I know will bless you and help you to grow daily in His favor:

Decree them out loud as you finish this book and every day from now.[2]

'God's Favor is on me Today'

'I am Blessed and Highly Favored! I live in Increase and Overflow.

'I call in Supernatural Favor and Full Restoration'

'My best days are still in front of me'

'Favor, Favor, Favor goes before me and surrounds me like a Shield'

'I walk in the Fullness of the Favor of God NOW and every day'

APPENDIX 1

Favor Scriptures in the Bible

Genesis 4:5 (NIV)

…but on Cain and his offering he did not look with favor. So, Cain was very angry, and his face was downcast.

Genesis 6:8 (NIV)

But Noah found favor in the eyes of the Lord

Genesis 18:3 (NIV)

He said, "If I have found favor in your eyes, my lord, do not pass your servant by."

Genesis 33:8 (NIV)

Esau asked, "What's the meaning of all these flocks and herds I met?" "To find favor in your eyes, my lord," he said

Genesis 34:11 (NIV)

> Then Shechem said to Dinah's father and brothers, "Let me find favor in your eyes, and I will give you whatever you ask.

Genesis 39:21 (NIV)

> the Lord was with him; he showed him kindness and granted him favor in the eyes of the prison warden

1 Samuel 2:26 (NIV)

> And the boy Samuel continued to grow in stature and in favor with the Lord and with people

2 Samuel 2:6 (NIV)

> May the Lord now show you kindness and faithfulness, and I too will show you the same favor because you have done this.

2 Chronicles 33:12 (NIV)

> In his distress he sought the favor of the Lord his God and humbled himself greatly before the God of his ancestors

Esther 2:9 (NIV)

> She pleased him and won his favor. Immediately he

provided her with her beauty treatments and special food.

Esther 2:15 (NIV)

Esther won the favor of everyone who saw her

Esther 5:19 (NIV)

If the king regards me with favor and if it pleases the king to grant my petition and fulfill my request

Nehemiah 5:19 (NIV)

Remember me with favor, my God, for all I have done for these people

Nehemiah 13:31 (NIV)

I also made provision for contributions of wood at designated times, and for the first fruits. Remember me with favor, my God

Job 11:19 (NIV)

You will lie down, with no one to make you afraid, and many will court your favor

Psalm 5:12 (NIV)

Surely, Lord, you bless the righteous; you surround them with your favor as with a shield

Psalm 45:12 (NIV)

The city of Tyre will come with a gift, people of wealth will seek your favor

Psalm 77:7 (NIV)

"Will the Lord reject forever? Will he never show his favor again?

Psalm 84:9 (NIV)

Look on our shield, O God; look with favor on your anointed one

Psalm 85:1 (NIV)

You, Lord, showed favor to your land; you restored the fortunes of Jacob

Psalm 89:17 (NIV)

For you are their glory and strength, and by your favor you exalt our horn

Psalm 102:13 (NIV)

> You will arise and have compassion on Zion, for it is time to show favor to her; the appointed time has come.

Psalm 106:4 (NIV)

> Remember me, Lord, when you show favor to your people, come to my aid when you save them,

Proverbs 3:4 (NIV)

> Then you will win favor and a good name in the sight of God and man

Proverbs 3:34 (NIV)

> He mocks proud mockers but shows favor to the humble and oppressed

Proverbs 8:35 (NIV)

> For those who find me find life and receive favor from the Lord

Proverbs 11:1 (NIV)

> The Lord detests dishonest scales, but accurate weights find favor with him

Proverbs 10:32 (NIV)

> *The lips of the righteous know what finds favor, but the mouth of the wicked only what is perverse.*

Proverbs 11:27 (NIV)

> *Whoever seeks good finds favor, but evil comes to one who searches for it*

Proverbs 12:2 (NIV)

> *Good people obtain favor from the Lord, but he condemns those who devise wicked schemes*

Proverbs 13:15 (NIV)

> *Good judgment wins favor, but the way of the unfaithful leads to their destruction*

Proverbs 16:15 (NIV)

> *When a king's face brightens, it means life; his favor is like a rain cloud in spring*

Proverbs 18:22 (NIV)

> *He who finds a wife finds what is good and receives favor from the Lord*

Proverbs 19:6 (NIV)

> Many curry favor with a ruler, and everyone is the friend of one who gives gifts

Proverbs 19:12 (NIV)

> A king's rage is like the roar of a lion, but his favor is like dew on the grass.

Proverbs 28:23 (NIV)

> Whoever rebukes a person will in the end gain favor rather than one who has a flattering tongue

Isaiah 61:2 (NIV)

> to proclaim the year of the Lord's favor and the day of vengeance of our God, to comfort all who mourn,

Lamentations 4:16 (NIV)

> The Lord himself has scattered them; he no longer watches over them. The priests are shown no honor, the elders no favor

Ezekiel 36:9 (NIV)

> I am concerned for you and will look on you with favor; you will be plowed and sown

Daniel 1:9 (NIV)

> Now God had caused the official to show favor and compassion to Daniel

Daniel 9:17 (NIV)

> "Now, our God, hear the prayers and petitions of your servant. For your sake, Lord, look with favor on your desolate sanctuary

Zechariah 11:10 (NIV)

> Then I took my staff called Favor and broke it, revoking the covenant I had made with all the nations.

Matthew 20:20 (NIV)

> Then the mother of Zebedee's sons came to Jesus with her sons and, kneeling down, asked a favor of him

Luke 1:30 (NIV)

> But the angel said to her, "Do not be afraid, Mary; you have found favor with God

Luke 2:14 (NIV)

> "Glory to God in the highest heaven, and on earth peace to those on whom his favor rests."

Luke 2:52 (NIV)

> *And Jesus grew in wisdom and stature, and in favor with God and man*.

Luke 4:19 (NIV)

> *to proclaim the year of the Lord's favor*

John 5:32 (NIV)

> *There is another who testifies in my favor, and I know that his testimony about me is true*

Acts 2:47 (NIV)

> *praising God and enjoying the favor of all the people. And the Lord added to their number daily those who were being saved.*

Acts 7:46 (NIV)

> *who enjoyed God's favor and asked that he might provide a dwelling place for the God of Jacob*

2 Corinthians 6:2 (NIV)

> *For he says, "In the time of my favor I heard you, and in the day of salvation I helped you." I tell you, now is the time of God's favor, now is the day of salvation*

James 4:6 (NIV)

But he gives us more grace. That is why Scripture says: "God opposes the proud but shows favor to the humble."

Revelation 2:6 (NIV)

But you have this in your favor: You hate the practices of the Nicolaitans, which I also hate.

APPENDIX 2

Favor Decrees[1]

'God's Favor is on me Today'

'Favor goes before me and surrounds me like a Shield'

'I am Blessed and Highly Favored! '

'I call in Supernatural Favor and Full Restoration'

'My best days are still in front of me'

'I walk in the Fullness of the Favor of God NOW and every day'

'Today I will experience unprecedented favor and opportunities like I never have before'*

'The favor of God is about to manifest in my life and will turn the hardest times into the best times!'*

'I have favor and success, not because of my works, but because I believe Jesus made me righteous and earned them for me' *

'I choose to position myself in God's Favor today and every day'

'I expect God's favor in my life'

'TODAY is the day of God's favor for my life'

'Favor is NOW!'

APPENDIX 3

Your Salvation Prayer Today

Today is the day of your salvation!

Not only does 2 Corinthians 6:2 says Today is time of God's Favor, but it also tells the need for you to get right with God and give your life to Jesus Christ TODAY

> *For he says, "In the time of my favor I heard you, and in the day of salvation I helped you." I tell you, now is the time of God's favor,* **now is the day of salvation**

Jesus Christ loves you. He loves you so much that He died for you. He took your place, your sins, your consequences and penalty and gave you forgiveness, love and eternal life.

It is time to surrender your life to Jesus and receive His free gift of salvation.

If you have never asked Christ to take control of your life as your Lord and Savior –

Pray this prayer out loud-

> Lord Jesus Christ...
>
> I admit that I have sinned against you.
>
> I have lived for other things including myself and you have not been first in my life.
>
> Forgive me Jesus for all the things I have done.
>
> Thank you for loving me so much that you died for me and took the consequences of all my sins.
>
> I believe that you died and rose again and are alive so I can be set free from my sins and live in freedom today.
>
> I invite you to come into my life and take control.
>
> I accept your free gift of salvation by faith.
>
> I choose to live for You from this day forward.
>
> In Jesus name,
>
> Amen

Congratulations.

Today – You are now born again to live for Jesus Christ!

Today – You have been saved to live your life for Him from

this day forward.

Today - is the day of your salvation!

Endnotes

Introduction

(1) Deuteronomy 32:10 -

..he guarded him as the apple of his eye

Chapter 1

(1) Emirates Airlines are carriers of United Arab Emirates. They are owned by the government of Dubai and are part of the Emirates Group based in Dubai. They are the largest airline in the Middle East.

(2) The Iran – Israel War was from 13 June – 25 June 2025. It is also known as the Twelve -Day War.
https://en.wikipedia.org/wiki/Iran–Israel_war

Chapter 2

(1) Key aspects of God's favor – Google AI search

- Unmerited grace:

Favor is a gift, not something earned through performance or good deeds. It flows from God's love, mercy, and grace.

- Divine assistance:

It is described as supernatural help that can bring blessings, breakthroughs, and victories.

- Protection and promotion:

Favor acts like a shield, offering protection and leading to preferential treatment and promotion.

- Activated by faith:

The favor of God is often activated through faith, prayer, and confessing His promises.

- Connection to the heart:

The Hebrew word for "favor" can mean pleasure, delight, goodwill, and acceptance. It is associated with a heart that is perfect toward God, meaning it seeks His favor above all else.

(2) "The New Testament heightens the notion of favor by revealing that Jesus Messiah embodies divine favor toward humanity" – Bible Hub – Favor of God defined https://biblehub.com/q/what_does_god's_favor_mean.htm

(3) Middle English word for 'Comfort' - "strength, support, encouragement" (late 14c.). https://www.etymonline.com/word/comfort

(4) Pastor Bob Gass was the author of The Word For

Today - a free, daily devotional written by him from 1991 to 2019 and published around the world by United Christian Broadcasters (UCB).

(5) The saying "be careful what you wish for" originates from Aesop's Fables, a collection of moral tales from ancient Greece

Chapter 3

(1) The Greek word for 'Substance' in Hebrews 11 is Hupostasis

Strong's Concordance #5287 – hupostasis - to place or set under. In general, that which underlies the apparent, hence, reality, essence, substance; that which is the basis of something, hence, assurance guarantee, confidence (with the ob. sense).

https://www.hopefaithprayer.com/faith-hebrews-hupostasis/

Chapter 4

(1) Fuller Theological Seminary is an evangelical seminary founded in 1947 in Pasadena, California, United States. It has three Schools. The most well-known is the School of World Mission. C. Peter Wagner was the Professor of Church Growth from 1970 – 2001. Robert Clinton was the Professor of Leadership from 1981 – 2016

(2) Definition from Dictionary.com web-based service owned by IXL Learning that uses a proprietary dictionary

based on the Random House Dictionary Unabridged version 2001

(3) Ibid

Chapter 5

(1) Iris Ministries (now Iris Global) is a missionary organization founded in 1980 by Heidi and Rolland Baker. See https://www.irisglobal.org/history for more

Chapter 6

(1) Source of 'Pilgrimage' definition – University of York, United Kingdom. See https://www.york.ac.uk

Chapter 7

(1) Jerry Savelle – Walking in Divine Favor – Jerry Savelle Publications, 1997

(2) Jerry Savelle – The Favor of God– Publisher, Baker Publishing Group, 2012

(3) Ibid

Chapter 8

(1) 'Kairos' time - Kairos time is an ancient Greek term for a qualitative, opportune moment, rather than the quantitative,

ENDNOTES

linear passage of time. It is God's "right time" or a "set time" that is significant and meaningful. It is often associated with a moment of opportunity, spiritual insight, or divine purpose.

(2) Harvest International Ministries – H.I.M. – is an international Apostolic Network of 5-fold ministries dedicated to advancing the Kingdom of God by equipping leaders, multiplying churches, evangelizing, and bringing revival and reformation to the nations. It has over 25,000 members in over 65 nations. See https://www.harvestim.org

(3) Bruce Lindley - 'Fathering a Destiny' will help you discover your God-destiny as you grow the destiny of others. You will learn how to position in your destiny and give you a next-generation mindset. Published by ARC Global Australia in 2009. Order from Amazon Australia. See https://www.amazon.com.au

(4) Cheryl Lindley - 'An Army Arising to Shift the Nations' is a strategic tool for every believer that will change the way you pray and cause your prayers to impact and change nations. Revised Edition Published by ARC Global Australia in 2021 Order from Amazon Australia. See https://www.amazon.com.au

Conclusion

(1) Acts 10:24-35 -

> *"I now realize how true it is that God does not show favoritism but accepts from every nation the one who fears him and does what is right."*

Everyone is God's favorite.

Appendix 2

(1) Decrees marked with a * are from the teaching of Jerry Savelle from Jerry Savelle Ministries International. See www.jerrysavelle.org

Contact and Resource Details

Resources by Bruce and Cheryl Lindley

Fathering a destiny – Growing spiritual sons and daughters – Bruce Lindley

This leadership book on the apostolic fathering reformation will give you a next-generation mindset and help you discover your God-destiny as you grow the destiny of others. You will learn how to position in your destiny.

Encountering the Supernatural – Bruce Lindley

Encountering the Supernatural will take you on a journey to learn how to live in the supernatural daily as you learn how to build an atmosphere of the supernatural. Get ready to encounter a whole new realm of the supernatural.

The Seeing Transformation – Bruce Lindley

The Seeing Transformation will help you unlock your seeing so remarkable miracles will become your everyday reality.

May you receive an impartation of faith, revelation, an anointing in the realm of God perception and vision and a doorway into a brand-new realm of discovery in anointed and fulfilled Kingdom life.

The Father's Love – An encounter with God the Father – Bruce Lindley

The Father is waiting for you with open arms! There is a dimension of his love that most people have really experienced- let alone living. This Book includes practical activations and decrees that will help you have an encounter with the father's love.

A Whole New Era – Emerging Apostles and Prophets Today – Bruce Lindley

Many prophets have declared a whole New Era has begun. It requires a radical change in how Apostolic and prophetic leaders think and act. This resource is an overview of a 2-day event that was run in Australia for emerging apostles or many years. It will equip you and help you function in this New Era.

Longevity in Leadership – How to Run the Race and Finish well – Bruce Lindley

Longevity in leadership is something every leader desires, but most leaders don't know how to experience it. This is a leadership book will inspire you and equip you to run your race and finish well. It will also help the next generation to run their leadership race well too.

CONTACT AND RESOURCE DETAILS

Cheryl Lindley's Book

An Army Arising to Shift the Nations

This is a strategic tool for every believer that will change the way you pray and cause your prayers to impact and change nations. James Goll said this book 'lifts the vision beyond personal perspective into a global strategy to shift entire nations through prayer that strike the mark.' This has been used by leaders in five nations to raise up an army of prayer warriors and shift their nation.

All these books are available at Amazon

See https://www.amazon.com.au

To contact Bruce and Cheryl Lindley to arrange speaking engagements or additional resources:

Email: admin@arcglobal.org

Connect with ARC Global

ARC Global is an international community of apostles and prophets who seek to:
- Rise up in this new apostolic era and wineskin
- Walk together in strategic relationships in community
- Build the Kingdom of God together
- Mobilise Prayer Movements in Australia and the nations
- Equip & send apostolic and prophetic teams to the nations
- Strategically transform nations together
- Father emerging next generation apostles and prophets

ARC Global is relationship-based new apostolic wineskin.

Many who are not apostles and prophets have asked if they could align with ARC Global even though they are not 5-fold ministers – the answer is Yes!

ARC CONNECT is open to ALL leaders who desire to build the Kingdom of God, regardless of your ministry and gifts.

To Connect with ARC Global and begin this ARC Global apostolic alignment journey with us:

Please go to our web page at **www.arcglobal.org** for more information

www.ingramcontent.com/pod-product-compliance
Lightning Source LLC
Chambersburg PA
CBHW072336300426
44109CB00042B/1640